KU-043-945

CONTENTS

CHAPTER 1

MAKING IT REAL

What we see at the movies seems real.

We see fantastic creatures and terrible disasters.

We visit other times and other planets.

SPECIAL EFFECTS

Frances Ridley

Copyright © ticktock Entertainment Ltd 2009

First published in Great Britain in 2009 by ticktock Media Ltd,
The Old Sawmill, 103 Goods Station Road, Tunbridge Wells, Kent, TN1 2DP

project editor and picture researcher: Ruth Owen
ticktock project designer: Simon Fenn

**With thanks to Ben Smith of Red Star Studio (3D Animation and CGI Effects) and
Mark Turner of MTFX Special Effects**
Thank you to Lorraine Petersen and the members of nasen

ISBN 978 1 84696 942 3 pbk

Printed in China

A CIP catalogue record for this book is available from the British Library.

Picture credits (t=top; b=bottom; c=centre; l=left; r=right):
c.BuenaVista/Everett/Rex Features: 11. Courtesy of Twentieth Century Fox/Bureau L.A Collection/Corbis: 22-23.
Everett Collection/Rex Features: 28, 29t. FOX ANNE MARIE/CORBIS SYGMA: 15. c.20thC.Fox/Everett/Rex Features:
4-5, 17b. Getty Images: 1, 18-19. Jonathan Hordle/Rex Features: 6. MTFX Special Effects: 16, 17tl, 17tr, 20-21.
PENNINGTON DONALD/CORBIS SYGMA: 24. Photos 12/Alamy: OFC. Neal Preston/CORBIS: 14. Red Star Studio:
8-9. Ronald Grant Archive: 10, 26, 27. Shutterstock: 2-3, 6 (background), 12, 26-27 (background). SNAP/Rex
Features: 29b. Touchstone Pictures/ZUMA/Corbis: 7. c.Universal/Everett/Rex Features: 13, 25, 31. www.jimusnr.com:
23t (inset), 23b (inset).

Every effort has been made to trace copyright holders, and we apologise in advance for any omissions. We would be pleased to
insert the appropriate acknowledgments in any subsequent edition of this publication.

Tornadoes rip through Los Angeles, USA, in the movie The Day After Tomorrow

We watch as people grow older or change into horrible monsters.

But these scenes are not real.

They are made using special effects.

CHAPTER 2

CRAZY CREATURES

Many movie creatures are puppets.

Yoda was a tiny alien creature in the *Star Wars* movies.

In the *Star Wars* movie, *A New Hope*, the Yoda character was a hand puppet.

Yoda

How can you tell that Yoda is a puppet?

Yoda's eyes blink very slowly.
Yoda's lips do not move in time with the words.

The Vogons are huge aliens in the movie *The Hitchhiker's Guide to the Galaxy.*

Each Vogon is half puppet, half body suit.

The Vogon's head is animatronic. This means it has electronic machinery inside. A puppeteer makes the face move by remote control.

Animatronic Vogon head

The Vogon's body is hollow. The actor inside makes the Vogon walk.

Many modern films have computer generated (CG) characters. Artists create these characters.

The artists collect information about the character.
They find out what the character should look like.
They find out how it should move and behave.

First, an artist draws a sketch of the character.

A wire frame model is created on a computer.

The artists draw the character on paper. Then the artists create the character on a computer screen.

The artists build the character up stage by stage.

The artist adds rough details to the model.

Then, fine details are added.

Computer generated characters are added to scenes after they have been filmed. The actors have to act with a character that isn't there.

This is a scene from *Harry Potter and the Prisoner of Azkaban*.

Buckbeak and Harry Potter

During filming, the actor, Daniel Radcliffe, had to pat a beak on a stick! The character Buckbeak was then added to the shot by computer.

Pip and Giselle in Enchanted

Trained animals and CG animals were used in
the *Harry Potter* movies and in *Enchanted*.

CHAPTER 3
STRANGE CHANGES

Make-up artists change the way actors look. They use effects such as fake blood and wigs.

Coloured contact lenses

Make-up

False teeth

In the movie *Evan Almighty,* the main character starts out with short hair and no beard.

He changes to a man with flowing white hair and a beard!

The actor had to wear 19 different wigs and 17 beards.

The make-up artist carefully planned each stage of the change.

The make-up artist used a technique called "flocking". He stuck beard hairs on one at a time. This made it look as if the beard was growing out of the actor's face.

Actor Steve Carell in *Evan Almighty*

Make-up artists use prosthetic make-up to create some effects. Masks and fake noses are both types of prosthetic make-up.

To make a prosthetic mask the make-up artist first makes a plaster mould of the actor's face.

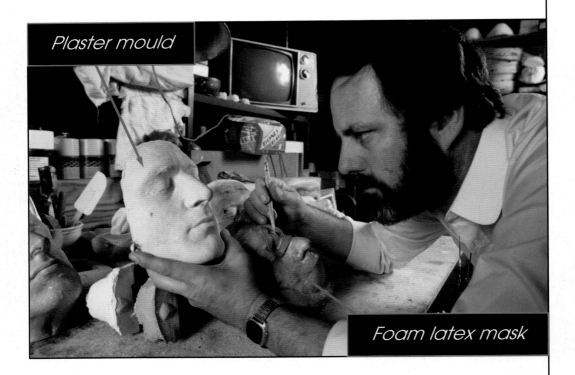

Plaster mould

Foam latex mask

The mould is used as a base to make a rubbery mask from foam latex. Effects such as scars, lumps and warts can be added to the mask!

Then the mask is glued to the actor's face.

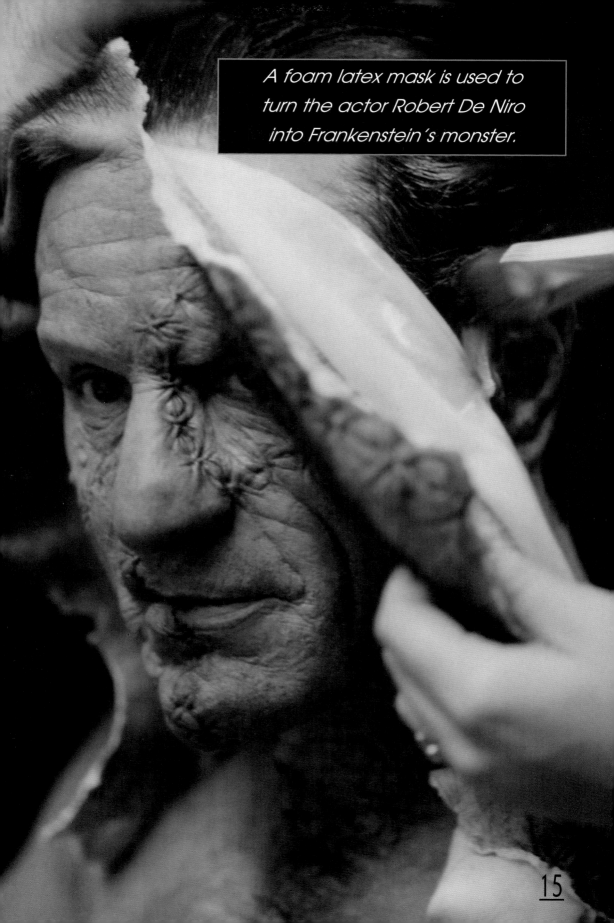

A foam latex mask is used to turn the actor Robert De Niro into Frankenstein's monster.

CHAPTER 4 : BURNING BUILDINGS

Many action movies have fires and explosions. It's dangerous to start a real fire on a film set. So, special effects are used instead.

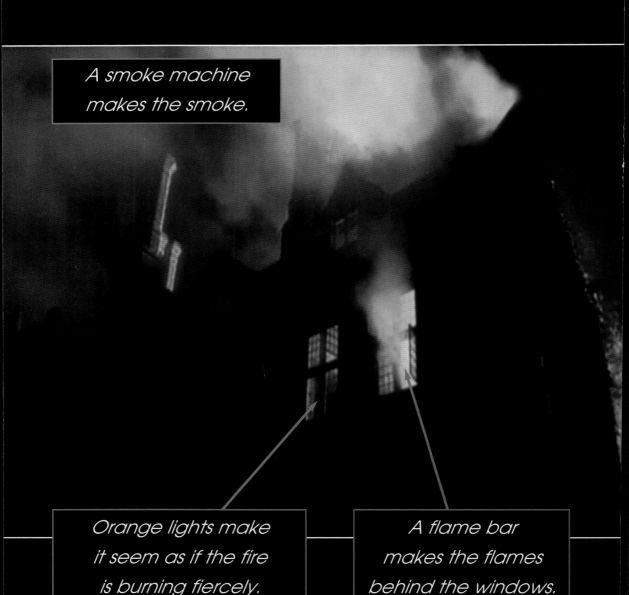

A smoke machine makes the smoke.

Orange lights make it seem as if the fire is burning fiercely.

A flame bar makes the flames behind the windows.

Flame bar

Smoke machine

A flame bar is a tube with holes in it. Gas bottles pump gas into the flame bar. Then the gas is set alight to make a flame effect.

The Towering Inferno

Many scenes are filmed using models instead of real buildings or cars.

The burning skyscraper in the movie *The Towering Inferno* was a 21-metre-high model.

Special effects fires and explosions can be dangerous. They can also be very expensive.

Many modern movies now create these effects on a computer.

The movie *Pearl Harbor* has scenes of fighter planes and explosions.

Some of the planes and explosions were real and some were computer generated.

Most movie-goers can't tell the difference!

Pearl Harbor

CHAPTER 5

STORMY WEATHER

Special effects teams often have to make the right weather for a movie.

Wind machine

A giant fan called a "wind machine" is used to make a gale.

A "rain stand" makes a rain effect.

A rain stand is like a big garden sprinkler. It's connected to a pump which is attached to a large container of water.

The pump pushes water through the rain stand at high pressure.

Some movie weather is really extreme!

In the movie *The Deluge*, New York is hit by
a tidal wave. The movie was made in 1933.

The special effects team built a huge model of New York.
Then they tipped tanks of water onto the model.

There is a tidal wave scene in *The Day After Tomorrow*.

The Day After Tomorrow

The Day After Tomorrow was made in 2004.

The special effects team scanned 50,000 photos of New York into a computer. The photos were used to make a digital model of the city.

Then the city was destroyed by a digital wave!

A model of New York is covered in water in the movie The Deluge.

CHAPTER 6

SETTING THE SCENE

Movies can be set in castles, spaceships or on boats. The 1997 movie *Titanic* was set onboard a giant ocean liner.

The special effects team built a scale model of the Titanic. The model is one twentieth of the size of the real ship. It is almost 14 metres long.

The model took 65 model makers almost five months to create.

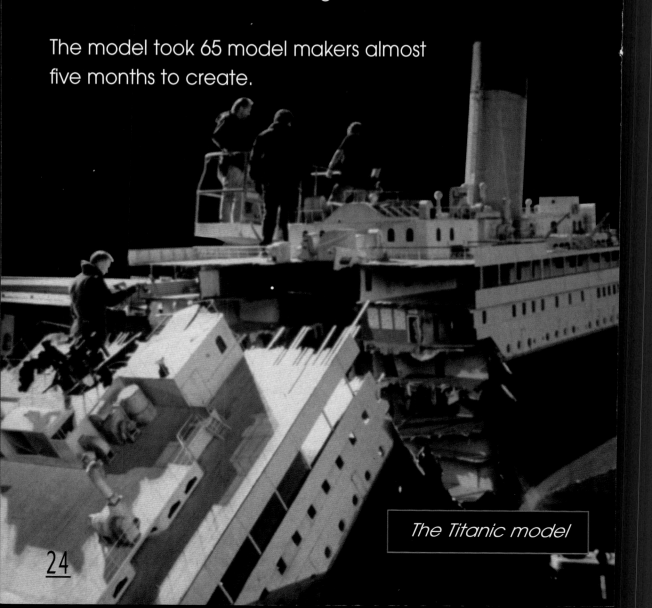

The Titanic model

In the movie *Evan Almighty,* God tells the main character to build a giant boat, or ark – just like Noah does in the Bible.

The movie-makers built an ark that was the same size as the ark in the Bible!

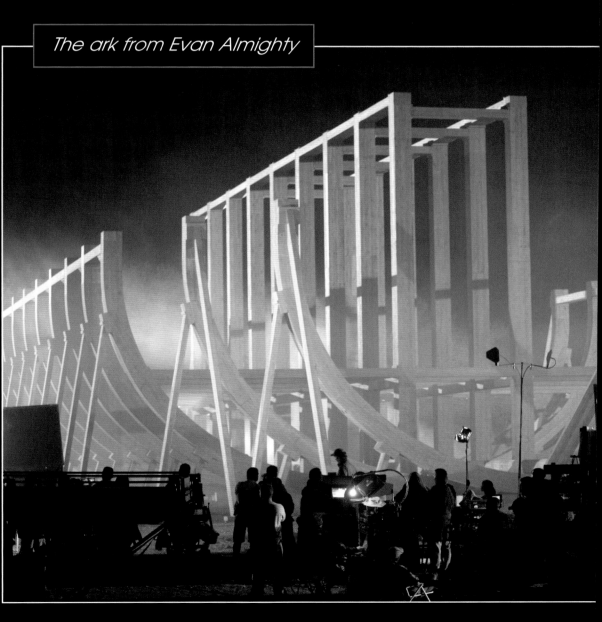

The ark from Evan Almighty

The background scenery in movies is often not real. It can be a painted scene, or a scene created on a computer. This is called matte painting.

In the past, backgrounds were painted on to glass. Then the painting was filmed.

The actors were filmed against a blue background.

Then the two films were put together to make one piece of film.

Blue screen background

In modern films, the backgrounds are created on a computer.

The actors are filmed against a blue or green screen.

Then the two images are put together using a computer.

Computer generated background

CHAPTER 7

MORE SFX MOMENTS

1895 - THE EXECUTION OF MARY, QUEEN OF SCOTS

This movie featured the first ever special effect.
In the movie, the queen has her head cut off.
A dummy was used for the beheading scene.

1933 - KING KONG

This was the first *King Kong* movie. The special effects team used a model gorilla, model sets and a doll.

1963 - JASON AND THE ARGONAUTS

Fighting skeletons were brought to life using stop-motion in this movie. Lots of photographs were taken of the models at different stages of movement.
Then, the pictures were run together
very fast.

1977 - CLOSE ENCOUNTERS OF THE THIRD KIND

In this movie, a giant alien spaceship lands on Earth. The spaceship was actually a two-metre-wide model.

1995 - TOY STORY

Toy Story was the first completely computer generated movie.

NEED TO KNOW WORDS

animatronic Puppets that have electronic machinery inside them. A puppeteer makes the puppet move by remote control.

character A person, animal or creature in the story of a film, book or TV show.

computer generated (CG) Something that is created on a computer. A computer artist puts information about a character or background into a computer. The artist then creates a picture of the character or background on screen.

contact lens A small piece of plastic that is put on the surface of the eye. Contact lenses help people to see clearly. Some contact lenses are in different colours. They can change the colour of the eyes.

digital model A picture on a computer screen that looks 3D.

foam latex A man-made material that can be moulded easily when it is wet. Special effects make-up artists use it to make masks and to create 3D make-up effects.

prosthetic make-up 3D make-up that changes the shape of an actor's face or body.

puppeteer A person who makes a puppet move.

scale model A copy of an object that is smaller than the real object.

scene A small part of a film that is set in one time and place. When the time and place changes, another scene begins.

set The background in a movie or TV scene. For example, it might look as if the actors in a movie are in their kitchen at home. In fact, the kitchen is a set that has been built in a movie studio.

technique A way of doing something.

SPECIAL EFFECTS FIRSTS

• The first ever Academy Award, or Oscar, for make-up was given in 1981. It went to special effects make-up artist Rick Baker. He won it for his work on the movie *An American Werewolf in London*.

• The first movie to include a fully CG character was *Young Sherlock Holmes*. The movie was made in 1985. The CG character is a knight who is part of a stained glass window. The knight comes to life and jumps out of the window.

• The first movie to use live actors and all CG sets was *Sky Captain and the World of Tomorrow*. It was made in 2004.

An American Werewolf in London

SPECIAL EFFECTS ONLINE

Websites

http://www.pbs.org/wgbh/nova/specialfx2/
Includes a special effects timeline and glossary

http://videos.howstuffworks.com/reuters/3358-beowulf-3-d-technology-video.htm
Videos showing how special effects are created

INDEX